Yesterday's Main Streets

the poetry of
ayaz daryl nielsen

ISBN: 978-81-19228-95-9

First Edition: 2023
Rs. 200/-

Cyberwit.net
HIG 45 Kaushambi Kunj, Kalindipuram
Allahabad - 211011 (U.P.) India
http://www.cyberwit.net
Tel: +(91) 9415091004
E-mail: info@cyberwit.net

Printed at Vcore.

To write
includes lives, includes life
creates
arched necks upon cloudberry
and pomegranate poetics
striking
as if stones from the sky
earth
as it responds
with the thrum
of
our being.

young woman next door
gently crooning
Russian lullabies

people pass by
a dog
waiting for dog

crossroads-
another year
beginning to end

upon the shelf
of a redwood bay window
used Harley parts
sutra of yearning
we all sigh
in unison

asking grandfather
about spirit as we rest
within warmth from his
cast iron wood stove
"your grandmother,"
he replies, "and a path
through the forest"…

walking meditation
the sway of her hemline
as she moves

yesterday's main streets
left behind…
forgotten somethings

crow on a branch
dissing the noisy mutt
so beneath him

nighttime movement
among the saguaro- - zephyr,
ghost or trickster?

Everything exists within original rhythms
Snarks and those quarks even goodnight kisses
The enactment of aeons and footfalls of ancients
Everything exists within original rhythms
Within a long wait for morning
Within the yearning for home
Everything exists within original rhythms
Snarks and those quarks even goodnight kisses

aster and pasque
the weight
of dewdrops

Aunt Enid's phone calls
lovely birthday greetings each
and every new season

thick wallet
filled with sticky notes- -
unfinished poems

lovely eyelashes
Spring flowers of
the grama grass

meditating before breakfast
already
egg on my face

when being embraces
what pages can give
black within white
and white within black
harmonies beyond
absolute certainties

in the evenings
glow of butterfly
songs of whippoorwills
promises of
early morning light

mountains beyond
snow-covered mountain
sunset into sunsets

wasp nests and prayer flags
quiet co-existence
beneath one roof

86'd
the party stopped
I didn't

his graveside service
three pall-bearers
a defrocked priest
and an x-wife's
hangover
up
and
over
July sunshine
August rain
a climbing vine
with purple blossoms

homeow

Autumn
summer's
grey hair

overnight rain
glides under the bridge
an older me
whom failures abandoned
no longer
the troubled guest,
a rain-fed acolyte,
a follower of rivers

the whispers from rain
upon window and doorstep
early morning's new hymns
upon our closed eyes

before our rest
the light within
shared moments

young nephews
insisting shadows
need toilet paper

red and white roses
children on the playground
sun above all

snow flakes
across hot asphalt
tumbling dice

above the marsh
something birdish in the reeds
unseen wholesomeness

Tomorrow, I'll write the poem about clouds
Tomorrow, I'll work on the poem about clouds
Tomorrow, I'll finish the poem about clouds
Today I'll just rest and watch clouds.

One day we have snow
One day we have rain
One day we have ice
One day we have sun
One day we have wind
One day we have mist
One day we have clouds
The seven days of us

retired farm couple,
kinsfolk with visages
of worn acceptance
a tanned, modest wisdom

poets searching
the searing heat of
living and dreaming,
forming words from
pure burning coals
found within the
collective heart
of all being

I saw a lynx
above Gold Hill
deep in a restless night
when I should
have been sleeping
a quick flash
through headlights
and deep in
a restless nigh
above Gold Hill
the lynx saw me
unique courtesy
a poem with its kept secrets-
sudden swoop of words

Between you and I
even within silence
    everything

night-time movement
among the saguaro — zephyr,
phantom or trickster?
heavy wool blankets
this old house clinging to
a chill winter morning

to sin or not to sin

to kiss you,
perhaps a sin- -
not kissing you,
a greater sin- -
oh, lovely sinfulness!

morning breeze and
cottonwood seeds…
contemplating
the essence
of spirit

big bluestem,
mountain mahogany,
blue gramma grass, and
prickly pear cactus- -
and me, too! me, too!

moon and shadows
hiking boots and I
late night friends

As I awaken and stretch my arm upward
it feels as though the sky places
invisible palms upon mine
as I stretch my other arm downward
it feels as though the earth places
invisible palms upon mine… and
it's as though a new day already is
percolating absolutely everything.

Within Mystery

Within the glove on a hand
Within a leaf in the wind
Within a song unsung
Within a vow that's unbroken
Within the love for another
Within the end of a queue
Within the state of union
                    of joy
                    of birth
                    of grief
                    of death
                    of atonement
                    of each moment
                    of resurrection
Within a long wait for morning
Within the yearning for home
Immersed and certain within mystery

meditating
before breakfast- already
egg on my face

mountains beyond
snow-covered mountains
sunset into sunsets

'and shadows'
my young nephew insists
'need deodorant, too!'

a small cloud
crosses the moon
a single footprint
in melting snow…
soon

the smallest
pushed from the nest- -
what karma, this?

late evening fireflies
whippoorwills
and kisses

86'd
the music stopped
I didn't

Spring warmth
snoozing on soft grass
among tulips

aster, pasque,
and penstemon
the weight
of dewdrops

same new same full same
blue same crescent same gibbous
same romantic moon

the body part
nighttime mosquito bite
I sit on

mossy rock
a summer's day's
notions

late evening tremor- -
someone dares to
call me a poet?

and the
sun rises!...
kiss me

Everything exists within original rhythms
Snarks and those quarks even goodnight kisses
The enactment of aeons and footfalls of ancients
Everything exists within original rhythms
Within a long wait for morning
Within the yearning for home
Everything exists within original rhythms
Snarks and those quarks even goodnight kisses

red and white roses
children playing nearby
the sun above all

my day's screwup's
i must have forgotten my
big-person panties

Unholy Spirit

Un-sanctified,
engorged and
elevated by
thick black night,
weak and withered
by early morning's
light, the obvious,
constant and un-
wanted suitor

she lay aside her pen
the evening darkness in place
a quiet city

late evening labyrinth
a brown sheen upon the spell-
binding play of faces

and we dance,
dear one,
with nothing on
but love

years as a hospice nurse

I've forgotten your names
and the various illnesses
but always, a lasting grace

whispers of rain
upon roof and porch
morning sends
a hymn as we
open our eyes

inside the old shed
puddles of fresh wetness
as if the roof weeps

young niece, asking
each and every rose
"Will you marry me?"

no, morning breeze…
you cannot have
her lingering scent

www.ingramcontent.com/pod-product-compliance
Lightning Source LLC
Chambersburg PA
CBHW050027170726
48282CB00025B/577
* 9 7 8 8 1 1 9 2 2 8 9 5 9 *